WHEELCHAIR SAMURAI

Lee Rossi

Plain View Press
P.O. 42255
Austin, TX 78704

plainviewpress.net
pk@plainviewpress.net
512-441-2452

Copyright © 2011 Lee Rossi. All rights reserved under International and Pan-American Copyright Conventions. No part of this book may be reproduced or distributed in any form or by any means, or stored in a data base or retrieval system, without written permission from the author. All rights, including electronic, are reserved by the author and publisher.

ISBN: 978-1-935514-15-2
Library of Congress Number: 2010941028

Cover Illustration by Roger Shimomura

Cover design by Susan Bright

for the fam

Acknowledgements

Heartfelt thanks to Roger Shimomura for permission to use *Oriental Masterprint (No. 1)* on the cover of this book.

Poems in this collection have appeared in the following publications: "On Poverty," "The Night Man," "Elegy in an Elephant Graveyard," "Pantoumime," "*Perché No,*" "The Monk and the Killer Chickens" in *The Atlanta Review*; "To the Teenager I Nearly Hit on Fairfax" and "'I and the Village'" in *Beyond the Valley of Contemporary Poets, 2000*; "After Spicer" in *Blue Satellite*; "Leaving Tracks" in *The California Quarterly*; "Rockefeller's Teeth," "*Discobolos,*" "*Berliner Weisse,*" and "May Day, 1975" in *The Chariton Review*; "Song for the Millennium" in *Daybreak*; "Dust" in *~88~*; "Rocket 88" in *Epicenter*; "In the Nursery of Priests," "Letter To a Grandchild," and "Myopia" in *Green Hills Literary Lantern*; "The Grasshopper and the Ant" in *Heliotrope*; "A Poet" in *The Long Island Quarterly*; "Daddy Long Legs" & "Snake Skin" in *The MacGuffin*; "Fifth-Year Latin" in *Main Street Rag*; "Rene and the Fly" in *ONTHEBUS*; "'The Vulture Knows'" in *Mischief, Caprice, and Other Poetic Strategies* (Red Hen Press, 2004); "Mother Tongue" in *The Pacific Review*; "'Masculine, Summer, Wet'" in *PoetryBay*; "Mantis in Spring," "The Matter of the Caterpillar," "The Sauna" and "The Road to Emmaus" in *Poetry East*; "Underwood" in *Poet Lore*; "The Ghetto Tree" in *Pool*; "Underground" in *Rattle*; "'Figure with Meat'" in *Rhino*; "The Final Chapter of the Novel Has Been Suppressed" and "Space Walk with Turkeys" in *Slipstream*; "Yakuza in the Jacuzzi" in *The Southeast Review*; "In the Sculpture Garden" in *The Southern Indiana Review*; "Borrowed Light," "'Philip Sleeping'" and "Spelling Bee" in *The Southern Poetry Review*; "Camping on the Big Sur" in *Spoon River Poetry Review*; "Early Space Travel," "Eclipse" and "Lessons in Sushi" in *The Sun*; "Almost Icarus" in *The Tampa Review*; "When I Lost It" and "The Great Circle" in *Tar River Poetry* and "Mantis in Spring" at *Blue's Cruzio Cafe* (www.cruziocafe.com).

Contents

Blood Litany   7

Underwood	9
Eclipse	10
The Night Man	12
Yakuza In the Jacuzzi	14
Elegy In an Elephant Graveyard	16
The Grasshopper and the Ant	18
Perché No	20
Dust	23
Song For the Millenium	25
"The Vulture Knows"	27
Scavenger Hunt	29
A Poem by Dean Young	31
The Ghetto Tree	32
When I Lost It	33
"The Final Chapter Of the Novel Has Been Suppressed"	34
May Day, 1975	36
Berliner Weisse	38
Underground	39

A Boy's Gift for Error   41

Borrowed Light	43
Spelling Bee	44
"Masculine, Summer, Wet"	45
To the Teenager I Nearly Hit On Fairfax	46
Rocket 88	48
Mantis In Spring	49
Myopia	50
A Habit Of Ascent	51
René and the Fly	53
Fifth-Year Latin	54
The Grove	55
Yellow Jacket	56
In the Nursery Of Priests	57
The Sauna	58
Snake Skin	59
Leaving Tracks	60
The Great Circle	61
Early Space Travel	62

Letter To a Grandchild   63
Daddy Long Legs   64
Camping On the Big Sur   65
The Matter Of the Caterpillar   66

Recipes For the Afterlife   67

Pantoumime   69
Sadao S. Munemori Memorial Interchange   70
The Road To Emmaus   71
Space Walk With Turkeys   72
On Poverty   74
Lessons In Sushi   75
Mother Tongue   77
After Spicer   78
A Poet   79
Almost Icarus   81
Every Anger Has a Voice   83
The Monk and the Killer Chickens   84
"I and the Village"   86
"Figure With Meat"   87
"Philip Sleeping"   88
Discobolos   89
"Rockefeller's Teeth"   90
In the Sculpture Garden   92

About the Author   95

BLOOD LITANY

Underwood

All afternoon we cast *bocce* balls toward the purgatory pit
at alley's end, the air a minestrone of milkweed & pollen.

Like a choir of nuns, mosquitoes hummed their blood litany,
while the adults sipped tumblers of Jack around a nicotine campfire.

Kids, adults, I was tired of them both and sought refuge
indoors in the cool murk of Aunt Baby's office.

Was she really Personal Assistant to the President
of Southern Bell? How silly she sounded, giddy with booze.

Not like the room, spare, the bookshelves barely inhabited,
a manual typewriter on the heavy wooden desk.

Its keys were blank, unlabeled, buoyant as storm clouds
with possibility. I pressed them singly, testing their weight.

I was the kid at a carnival who swings
the heavy mallet trying to ring the bell.

And I was Adam naming the wolf and the boar,
and taping its name to its hide.

And when after hours of pecking and hunting,
I showed my aunt, she marveled, disarming me with praise,

afraid, perhaps, that when combined, those letters
might transcribe the molecules of the future, and I, boy

alchemist, might uncover other secrets, the sadness of adults,
how everyone betrays the child she used to be.

Eclipse

After the 4th course and 5th bottle of wine,
my wife, my friends, & I stumbled onto
the porch, just in time to see Earth
take its first bite of the moon's mottled *bleu*.

Someone said the full moon always
reminded him of a guy with bad acne,
Tommy Lee Jones perhaps.
I said it reminded me of my boss,

the pocked inventor of the tetrahedral spike,
a clever little gadget
you could drop from an unseen B-52
into rice paddies miles below

and which always landed point up
ready to pierce boot, sandal or naked foot.
He was proud to have served his country
in such a demonstrably harmful way.

I wondered if the moon was disappearing
in Vietnam as well. Total eclipses are local events
like divorce and heart attack. Maybe
they were just having a chest cold over there.

That's when I mentioned the murdered woman.
She'd lived in the next apartment with her husband
or boyfriend, whatever he was. They were both refugees.
At night my wife and I would lie in bed and listen

to her body slam against our bedroom wall.
Next day she'd say they were discussing their future.
I heard my wife telling about the murder,
things police want to know,

who gave him the gun, how he tracked her down,
why we didn't report the beatings.
Not why it's easier to see the big picture –
millions of kilotons, millions of casualties,

or why when you're that close to suffering
you often look away.
The dance of planets continued
until the eclipse was full.

The darkened moon didn't look like cheese anymore
or someone's cratered face but like an innocent rock
hurled from who knows what distance
at some unsuspecting target.

The Night Man

His Old Spice floats like a skiff
on the sicky sweet of spilt beer.
From 4 until after midnight,
the fat-bellied decanters wear him like a smear
as he dispenses drinks, patrols the duckboards,
nails groaning like prisoners in stockade,
wipes up spills and the tiny reflecting pools
left by bottle and glass. A dandy
in his fresh white shirt and sharply creased slacks,
he serves a brotherhood of bachelors:
the tax guy whose pale plush hands cost him
all his girlfriends, the building inspector
whose neck swells like an inflatable hemorrhoid cushion.
For one, dinner is a jar of fluorescent cherries,
for another, it's olives with their gallstones removed.

Pundit of the potable, savant of the sipped,
he knows all the recipes for disaster.
With gin and soda, lemon juice and sugar,
he'll tell the tale of Tom,
miscreant and heir to the Collins fortune,
who in one night visited all the pubs in London,
only to greet the new day surrounded by
the graves of his forebears. Kahlua,
vodka and cream will set you on a wild charge
through forests of naked aspen
into the waiting guns of the Red Army.

From time to time he taps the metal plate above his right eye –
sound but no feeling – as if to remind himself of something.
You can take the whisky and vermouth tour
of the Big Apple or lose your head to the Virgin
Queen's older sister. Or with vodka and orange juice
open the lid of your father's coffin.
He listens to all the stories like someone in a wheelchair
watching swimmers being swept out to sea by an undertow.
But don't ask him to join you while he's on duty.

He's a pro. With a bat underneath the bar
for rummies who want a fight, a gun for stickup men.
And back in his room, a bottle of 90-proof.
Never mix, never worry, the lone incorruptible truth.
His own executioner, one shot at a time.

Yakuza In the Jacuzzi

I don't know what my sister sees in her mobster.
A casket full of money is my guess.
Ugly as a fireplug, he's almost as short.

Once when she was drunk, maybe it was
Buddha's birthday, she let slip
he was great in bed, a real Godzilla.

I don't want to think about it. I've seen him
floating like a walrus in the giant
redwood crockpot behind their house.

I know it's dumb – he could crush me like a puppy
in a trash masher – but I can't help teasing him.
"How do you say 'ugly' in Japanese?" I ask.

And he asks, "How you say 'stupid' in English?"
Maybe he tolerates me because
I'm her brother, and he loves her, even if

what he does for a living is bust kneecaps
and skulls with my old Louisville sluggers.
We're soaking in the hot tub, a killer whale

and a guppy circling a small lagoon,
and all I really want is to scrub away those awful tattoos
covering the drive-in movie screen of his back–

geishas with shotguns, samurai in wheelchairs,
Fuji-san about to blow its top
and drown Edo in a sea of fire.

Buddha says we're all struggling to break the cycle
of sin and rebirth, even the worst of us,
so maybe it's good that he has someone's love

to weigh against the evil of his life, but all
I can see is a 60-foot-lizard
flattening my sister like a cardboard city.

Elegy In an Elephant Graveyard

My children test the ooze at the Ice Age Museum
to see how hard it is to extricate
an arm (hard!) or a leg (harder!).

Outside, tar pits bubble and burp,
evidence that million-year-old ferns
still simmer in caldrons deep underground.

Imagine the poor Columbia Mammoth,
ten thousand pounds of organic grass-fed meat,
sinking helplessly in a seductive waterhole.

Pit 91 at Rancho La Brea held the skeletons
of a hundred and eighty-one individuals, adults & calves,
live tissue, not the rock-for-carbon fossils in other sediments.

Ten thousand years ago the hunter-gatherers of ancient
Mesopotamia domesticated wheat, the horse, and the ox.
In North America, the Pleistocene mega-fauna died out.

The only sizeable predator to survive was man. My children,
latter-day epigones of human adaptability
examine a wall glowing with hundreds of wolf skulls,

anonymous in their representative glory.
In the next hall, a motorized saber-tooth drives its oversized
incisors into the fleshy scalp of a giant sloth.

This individual portrait of death frightens
my daughter, who hobbles like a baby mastodon
to the safety of her mother's long legs.

Other families roam from one diorama to the next,
small herds grazing on tufts of fact. A crowd gathers
in front of a large mural – nearly naked surfers

toss atlatls and spears tipped with chert
at a mammoth foundering in a sea of golden grass,
its tusks more fanciful than any Alpine horn,

shofars trumpeting a silent fanfare of farewell.
Having eaten everything that was easily killed,
those early humans learned to do without

the great stupid beasts that once filled the prairies
and forests. Every day, they say, another species is lost.
Tonight my children will dream of beauties we've destroyed

to keep them alive. After lunch they spin down the park's
grassy slopes like asteroids in the giant fridge of space.
SUV's hunt for parking like wolves circling a flock of sheep.

The Grasshopper and the Ant

How they flock to me, pigeons to a gift of crumbs, as I step into the showroom, blinded by the gleam of metal and chrome. The sales manager introduces himself and his understudy, and I tell them I'm looking for something with a very small sticker price.

They both frown as if trying to imagine what sort of person would make such a rude and insensitive remark, but quickly restore that professional look of smiling inquisition on their faces. They've come from all over the world, Tim from Afghanistan, Mike from Iraq, Tony from Huntington Beach, to sell me a car. They're here to help me spend my money, like oral surgeons all working on my mouth at once.

"I'm a poet," I tell them, as we cruise the back lot looking for something cheap enough for my lack of pride and ambition. I'm doing what I can to fill the silence of their calculation – *isn't there some way to interest him in something with power door locks and a spoiler, how much interest will we have to charge to make money on this deal?*

I want to ask what they drive back home in Baghdad and Kabul, but think better of it. None of us needs to say what a bad year it's been for car sales, nor do I need to share what my dad, that eminent contrarian, always said, "Don't buy what they want you to buy."

It was my dad taught me to shop at the end of the model year, when inventory sticks in their wallets like over-the-limit credit cards. What he gave me was discipline and a healthy distrust of excitement.

But now I'm excited, full of the Novocain of ego. I've just bought the "manager's special," the car they don't want you to buy, so full of myself, I won't notice the pain until a month or two down the road. But for the moment, I'm jabbering like a cricket in a ditch, telling them how ugly their cars used to be (I drove one for ten years), and about my last car, a gift from my dad, sort of, how he only had it for a few months before his death.

Before turning the ignition for the first time, I sit and smell my new car. I can almost see my father that last summer in his garden, watching the peppers and garlic grow, watching the ants climb the tomatoes, and listening to the cicadas' shrill *pizzicati* and arpeggios, remembering, perhaps, his own personal summer, that ended so long ago, now that winter too was almost gone.

Perché No

Tourists are flowers that arrive full blown
to be placed in the vase of a *pensione*.
You see them at the station stepping off
the overnight from Munich, their wounded bags
plastered with bandages recalling the speed
and direction of their flight. Thus I mused,

and wondered what we were fleeing, my wife
and I. After a year instructing soldiers
at American bases, we were inspecting
those suspicious, nervous countries which called
themselves our allies. What should we do next,
we asked ourselves, since we had no one else
we trusted with our nerves or suspicions?

We spent our time in Florence shopping and
eating. We loved the outdoor leather market,
where you could buy shoes that fit like gloves, gloves
that fit like a caress, coats as soft as a lover's skin.
To tease our longing for transcendence, we
visited some famous paintings. The museum
smelled like a church, moldy and too sweet.

For sweet I preferred a particular *gelateria*,
its wickedly self-conscious name, *Perché No*,
so Henry James, as if for a moment
you might let yourself go: the labels as delicious
as the vividly colored ice: *Fragola*, the fugitive
taste of strawberry lips, *Malaga* where vines
swell with rain intoxicating as rum,
Tiramisu, which I dared mis-translate
as 'land where you lose yourself,' and *Tartufo*,
named for the scoundrel who traded on sanctity,
then seduced his host and benefactor's wife.

I chose Mr. T. in honor of the scoundrel
in myself. After our first visit we learned
to warm our tongues between bites
in order to suffer the penetrating cold,
the bold, biting flavors more deliciously.
Too much pleasure is its own kind of pain.
This, I thought, is what the afterlife would be
if God were Italian and not some ghost
radiating from a few old paintings.

Once we toured a tannery, where workmen
in goggles and waders scalded hides,
stripping hair, fat, and flesh. The place smelled
of death and metal salts, steam hovering over
flensing vats like the ghosts of the butchered,
reluctant to leave those cleverly knit
webs of protein which had contained their lives.
In the land of Dante and the Borgias
you can't spend all your time in Paradise.

Although it was not the slaughterhouse, I could
almost hear death screams and see blood streaming
from stricken throats. Walking from that squat prison,
our thoughts turned to the textures of Gucci,
the pleasantly contradictory taste of *zabaglione*.
It was the contrast between the delicious and the awful,
we told ourselves, that makes life interesting,
the vividness of taste and smell dispelling
that early morning numbness left by sleep.

We strolled among the ancient buildings,
their history of overheated love and betrayal
as palpable as their earth tones: umber
and ochre, orange and rust, elaborate

multi-story caves whose inhabitants hid
from neighbors and the curious. We felt
excluded from everything, forced to focus
on surface joys, our skins electric with
the static of our need. Surfaces betray,
we knew that, yet that was all we had,
unwilling to look beneath our own,
arresting gargoyles of desire and youth.

We passed a flower seller where bees circled
the flowers as if the flowers had invented bees.
"O Rose, thou art sick!" I wanted to say,
my mind consumed by the invisible Worm,
the one thing I could not say, until years
later when the leaves of that thorny bush
had been reduced to fragile, brilliant lace.

Tourists are like cut flowers. After a week
we begin to smell, and you throw us out.
I can still see that young couple of drunks
stumbling up twisting, cobbled streets, lips numb,
giddy with wonder and anticipation.
The night was warm, the air sweet with the smell
of leather, all those hairless skins, empty
now of their bodies, ready to wrap
anyone willing to pay the price.

Dust

The wall next door keeps rising
until finally it is all I can see.

From time to time I hear workmen
tapping the blocks
and singing beautifully in Spanish.

I step outside and there they are
six of them astride a scaffold slapping mud on top
or scraping excess from the sheer drop.
I admire their precision, pushing back space
with powerful rough hands.

And yet, rising even higher
surrounding this whole city
I see another wall.
Like insects through a hedge
we pass through it daily
finally without noticing its glittering green face.
Even as we sleep, it grows.

We are already destroyed
blonde bodies bundled in rolls
big as houses.

I cannot say who builds it.
I live as if the wall builds itself
its own father and mother.
It anchors heaven
lest God and Devil disappear.

I pray that it not fall.
I am not ready to leave this body
of theorem. I could not survive
in the black air of stars
nor enter the language of moss.

I am not ready to leave this body.
It is what I love,
the raised hand, this song
rising to a scream.

Song For the Millenium

At the end of the old century we knew the party was about to take
>   off. Crowds were gathering all around us, people from
>   Argentina & Peru & Germany & Tel Aviv & Bombay.
>   They were wearing grass skirts and dashikis and rags soaked in
>   gasoline. They were ready and they wanted to be party to
>   everything that happened on TV and in the papers and even
>   in video games. Everybody smiled except the guards standing
>   at the doors who had been trained not to smile but to stand
>   erect, backs to the doors, bright lights gleaming on their dark
>   glasses. I'm not saying this to criticize anybody. I love crowds.
>   I even love the guards . . . and you know I love a party.

Here we were – the biggest party in the history of the world –
>   skyscrapers burning like bonfires, freeways lit like rivers of
>   flame, klieg lights shining in the faces of millions. There was
>   music everywhere and whatever might pass for music – buses
>   braking, the crackling of telephones, comets passing planets
>   in close proximity, windows and doors slamming as people
>   leapt into the streets. Maybe it was all the music or else the
>   incredible wind carrying soot and smoke out of the hills into
>   the streets below, but something was not right. And all of a
>   sudden I felt as if I couldn't breathe and that nothing I was
>   seeing was real.

I wanted the party to stop. I wanted to open my door and walk into
>   my yard and watch hummingbirds at the feeder. But
>   helicopters kept circling and people started yelling, "not
>   enough . . . not big enough." The words came to me over
>   the shouts of DJs and TV reporters and messiahs in 3-piece
>   suits and all around me housetops caught on fire and
>   more and more people emptied into the streets demanding
>   truth and freedom and the company of angels and no-risk
>   high-return investments,

and then I woke, my entire body covered with soot, my tongue
and throat swollen, the smoke so thick I couldn't see, but I
raced downstairs anyway, flight after flight, the strength of my
fear and the vision of a door pulling me on, and when the
stairs just kept leading deeper and I did not reach bottom,
I let my fear take me further into darkness, the next landing
big as a train station and full of naked commuters, the guards
naked too, strapped to stacks of flaming computer printout,
the smoke so terrible everything blurred like on TV, and
so I went down finding fewer and fewer bodies, chicken bones
and feathers that were rocks and smells worse than
bubblegum, worse than gasoline.

I threw up dozens of times and pissed hard like a firehose for hours
flying low over houses and fires, trying to put them out slow
at first but then faster and faster in circles as big as the sun,
as big as the orbit of the sun, sick now, sick with fear of
hitting the ground and skidding for miles of being ground to
asphalt and hotdogs and dust, not even dust, not even ash or
atom, faint as the cosmic background radiation, the universe
a candle burning at 3 degrees above absolute zero before the
door of God.

"The Vulture Knows"

I'm a ghost. Sorry,
what I meant to say is,
I'm Lord of Hosts,
and, as such, smell
like a stinkbug, taste
like tobacco, flame
like a firefly, cackle
like dry brush, and caress
your tongue like a peach's
crushed velour. But
you can call me Chick.
You remember how
the crushed rosemary
on your mother's fingers
tasted like lightning.
Kennedy was President
and Berlin a place
surrounded by wasps.
By tanks. But what if
I'm not the Lord, and
what I said was Hostess,
not Hosts (an error
in transcription) –
cream-filled cupcakes
and Twinkies. The red light
of civilization depends
on getting this exactly right,
oder? Weift der Geier,
as my West German friends
used to say, whatever
they meant. How we loved to fly
like sparrows from one side
of the Wall to the other,
while the East Germans
sat in their guard towers,
benevolent, gently smiling
vultures. If you're still

reading, I'm sure you've
realized that the speaker
is not a messenger
of God's honest truth.
Doubtless he will spend
part of eternity
chewing baseballs for the
taste of horsehide. A goblin's
life for me, then, its
exquisite dastardy.
Better a medium oven
in hell, than the deep freeze
of inhibition. Or maybe not.
My cat, an avatar
of the Egyptian god
Osiris, smiles and says,
"Don't worry, kid,"
the ghost of wild tobacco
rising from his fur
like hillsides wet with fire.

Scavenger Hunt

The instructor was a deep-dish rhubarb pie.
(Well, maybe not deep, but certainly rhubarb.)
Even the thinnest slice left your tongue tingling.
Without (in most cases) a word of apology
we each placed a poem in the middle of the table
while the other students passed their hands above the page.
One poem turned into a donor organ, a liver,
ready for transplant. Another morphed into
someone's great grandmother's hat pin.
There was a sonnet that became a bucket
of dead roses, and quite a few headstones,
small and eaten by weather. There was
a gleaming petrochemical sunset and a car
in a cornfield resting on concrete blocks.
There was a girl with a wall-eye and a young son,
a couple of kids playing a twilight game of catch,
a couple in bed discretely covered by a blood-soaked
sheet, and an atom bomb looming over a tiny city
like a cobra, not to mention a dowsing stick,
a catalog of catalogs, a dimpled peasant doll
holding a cell phone, a plastic "tortoise shell"
compact with a cracked mirror, a forged
Gutenberg Bible, and a couple of strands
of viral DNA from the 1918 flu pandemic.

It was exhausting work, and eventually the whole
class fell asleep like townsfolk in a fairy tale.
That's when the pie changed into an old woman
made of copper tubing and sheet rock.
(Of course, I was asleep at the time, but my dream
seemed as real as anything that had come before.)
Slowly, so as not to wake anyone, she clanked
around the room and touched the students.
One became a meatloaf, one a hooded vulture,
one a priest. But she ran out of magic, don't ask
me why. When the meatloaf started scratching
his beard, the vulture noticed and ate him up.

The priest ducked under the table and kissed
the girls' kneecaps. But when everybody woke
(not everybody, we were a few bodies short),
there was nothing particularly strange or unusual
(we were used to the unusual, it was what we lived for),
just people with hangovers, staring at a vulture,
its beak and wattles slick with rhubarb.

A Poem by Dean Young

The reason why redheads, even the girls,
go bald is that they're missing a gene,
or is it a chromosome? Whenever a girl
smiles at me, I see a row of pearly white
tombstones. I prefer the stones at odd angles.
I like my graveyards lived in.
Have you ever seen a line of earrings
dangling from some girl's ear like straps
in a subway car? And haven't you wanted
to grab one, and hold on, just as the car
tipped full speed round the next curve?
Whenever cracks appear in the blast furnace
of my self-esteem, I know it's time for a new wife,
the ultimate insulating material.
If Dean Young looks real hard, he can see
the carbon atoms in his girlfriend's nose
as they formed under enormous pressure
in stars that exploded six billion years ago.
He always has a Kleenex handy.
Listen up, graduate assistants,
there's a dissertation waiting here.
Every couple of weeks Dean's
young friend jabs a needle in her arm,
flooding her Great Lakes with poison.
The shrubbery of Versailles
was Louis XVI's greatest poetry.
Queen Marie's slippers were galleons
of love, easily tipped in squalls of passion.
Whenever I take an RPG round
to the M-1 Abrams tank of my self-regard,
and the air's abuzz with microscopic particles
of radioactive doubt, I know I need to punch
a hole in some attractive woman's reserve.
Given my limited shelf life I grow
nervous at the approach of my pull date.
Nothing clears the air like 150 mm shells
packed with humor and charm.

The Ghetto Tree

I am the wet tree.
The *shtetl* girls don't want me.
All day their mothers tell them
what they don't want.
The man in the skyscraper
doesn't need glass or steel.
He thirsts for the wetness
of trees and a deep hole
in which to bury them.
If only the body wasn't a clock –
and the mind less of a freighter
crating perishables from one
hungry continent to another –
are they looking at me again?
With eyelashes sharp as hatchets?
One of them needs money.
Another needs an abortion.
They are singing for the man
on the 90th floor.
What do they need? My seed?
It is almost dawn.
Girls, walk out your door
and let my wet air, my wet, wet hair
tangle you in its tendrils.
If you want something better
than death, pick me.

When I Lost It

I was crossing a glassy stretch of middle age,
the farther shore still not quite visible,
when my mojo quit. My wife had turned gray,
my daughter was angry about her breasts,
and my son had wandered into a cornfield
and wouldn't come out. (I don't remember
what actually happened, this is just how it felt.)
I checked the gas tank, and though I'd been driving
for days, the tank was still full. I went to see my doctor.
He simply took it out (my mojo, that is), put it on
the examining table, poked it, walked around it,
slowly as if it were a piece of modern sculpture,
and said it looked fine to him. I felt better
when I left. Having it poked. Having the doc say
it looked okay. But it still didn't work.
My wife could tell you. Except she's too embarrassed.
So I took it to a plumber. He pounded it for hours.
Sent his snake all through it, replaced a bunch of pipes
with high-quality copper. Again I felt better,
like some test subject full of sugar pills.
But still no mojo. I called my friends,
who gathered around my bed. "I'm not dying,"
I said, "just . . . just . . . depleted, like a battery
or my bank account." Some said to eat less fat,
more roughage. Someone said I needed a vacation
at one of those all-naked resorts in Jamaica.
Judas said (there's always a Judas in every group),
she said I never had no mojo to begin with.
Maybe she was right. I stood up, or tried to –
I wanted to shove it in her face –
but couldn't remember where I put it.
Thank God for TV. Now that I've forgotten
how to stand (I'm not speaking literally, of course,
this is just how it feels), television is the only thing
I'm good at. I close my eyes and replay the story
of my life. I'm still editing – adding characters,
deleting birthdays, adding lots and lots of mojo.

"The Final Chapter of the Novel Has Been Suppressed"

In one ending Sir Stephen takes O on vacation to southern Sudan, and after sharing her with various tribal chieftains, sells her to the highest bidder. Before he can leave, she throws herself into the White Nile and is eaten by a crocodile.

In another ending, Stephen & O are driving to the chateau at Roissy when their cab is hit by a speeding milk truck. Stephen is killed, but O is taken to a hospital run by ecdysiast nuns and survives. After making a full recovery, she joins the order, and eventually becomes Mother Superior.

In another, she finds Sir Stephen violently fucking his brother René, her erstwhile lover, just like he used to fuck her. She rushes into Stephen's drawing room, scene of so many exquisite humiliations, loads his antique silver dueling pistols, walks back to the bedroom and shoots them both dead. At her trial, she is acquitted by reason of sodomy.

In still another, O leaves Stephen and gets a job as a waitress at a topless bar in a strip mall outside Phoenix, Arizona. She never gets over looking at other women's breasts or the pity she feels for the beads of sweat stranded like climbers beneath those trembling Alps.

Another finds her fleeing to Soho where she opens a tattoo and body piercing parlor. With the arrival of feminism, she converts it to a space for performance art, and transforms herself into the darling of the avant-garde, covering her own arms and legs in one breathtaking season with a colorful Henri Rousseau-inspired tapestry. She soon becomes one of Robert Mapplethorpe's favorite models, the tartan of welts and scars covering her buttocks among his most recognizable subjects.

In another, she offers herself as a guinea pig for a series of trials of anti-depressant drugs. She soon begins mixing her own anti-depressant cocktails. Before long, she has a string of pharmaceutical hits, and is named Director of Research for the largest drug company in the world. Then she discovers Viagra.

There are many more: Sir Stephen strangles O, the better to enhance his orgasm. O strangles Sir Stephen, the better to enhance his orgasm. O & Stephen get married, have kids, move to the suburbs of Phoenix. O gets fat. Goes on a diet. Shoots herself. Drowns the kids. Cuts off Stephen's dick.

There is no end to the story of O.

May Day, 1975

Somewhere one war was ending,
helicopters rising from the roofs of buildings
and spilling refugees like loose change,
while another war was blindly chipping
away at its prison with an egg tooth.

I was half a world away, sitting in the *Schloßpark*
and hoping for a visit from one of Rilke's angels.
Despite its name, there was no castle,
only a blank space in the middle of the city,
all that was left for the children of the firestorm.

I watched shoppers hurrying like Aeneas
into Hades and re-surfacing
from a cavernous underground grocery
with the heads of Demeter
and Eurydice in string bags,

and I wondered what the sudden beauty
of the sky, clouds like bolsters and featherbeds
lazing on a mattress all watery blue,
had to do with the uncharacteristic optimism
flooding me like snow melt.

Somewhere it was still winter,
the wind's serrated teeth gnawing
granite and gneiss,
but here the cherry trees unfurled
their fragrant labia.

And then across the vast green I saw a friend.
He was drunk and depleted, a soldier
who'd emptied his clip into the jungle,
frightened by something he couldn't see.
I could go home now and find my wife

alone for the first time in days.
I had given away something I didn't want
and now would have to take it back.
But I waited. Every year spring arrives
with its promise of less.

I waited for the angel to appear, waited
until the nimbus surrounding
everything faded and I was free
to step into a future
that even then was becoming my past.

Berliner Weisse

> *– 1976, West Berlin*

High above the *Grunewald* clouds floated
like lather in a basin. Or maybe it was
the second fishbowl of green beer
made it seem as if we were submerged

in a very large aquarium. We lay in the grass
beside the *Schlachtensee*, my hand an albino
tarantula crawling up my lover's arm
and into her hair. Charmed with our little getaway,

a weekend away from our homes, I was almost
inert, succumbing to the watery sky,
something I'd seen only in paintings
by Hals or Steen. How did jets rise in that

impossible atmosphere, banking over lakes and trees,
departing our lagoon of freedom, confined within
its concrete wall, guard towers and automatic guns.
Over the horizon, our spouses soldiered on

as if we were shopping for bread.
Floating in that sunken moment,
we were joined like some colony beast,
a jelly fish perhaps, or Man of War,

pushed great distances from ourselves
by currents that caressed with warmth
and only later smashed our happy adhoc union
against time's volcanic shore.

Underground

Like a caver edging along a narrow gallery
who must stoop, then crawl, then shimmy
like his ancestor snake through the narrowest
possible hole, I slid my fat boy, weeping
now in anticipation, between her cheeks
and pressed. It was someone else wearing
my name, my body. What kind of faith
pulls him into that unforgiving obstruc-
tion? Every day men get stuck in places
from which they can't withdraw, and suffer
those slow, painful deaths we like to imagine
only when we're warm and well-fed.
I'm not talking about mineral death,
of course, but the other kind,
where you're lying in bed with someone
you thought you wanted, and then realize
you don't. Most of the time, if he's careful
and lucky, the cave man slips through into a larger
chamber, a closet or vestibule. And once,
or maybe twice in a life, he'll find himself
in some immense opening, a cathedral
complete with organ pipes and carved
pillars soaring into the dark. I pressed again,
and she relaxed, allowing me to pop through
into that spacious underground, where
a man could lose direction and wander
until he'd forgotten why he wanted to leave.

A BOY'S GIFT FOR ERROR

Borrowed Light

You see those clouds? I wish the sky would swallow them
like dumplings. And the spaghetti strands left by jets,
those too. I don't care if the sky is just a bowl filled with static.
It has a job to do, clearing a space for night
so the moon can burst forth, a flower riding a stem of light,
parting the grave hours into the sea of departure and the sea of return.

Sun God and Moon Goddess, you remember them,
those silent-movie stars,
his purring convertible, her chauffeured limousine.
Do you think they still have gifts to give?
Who doesn't remember her warmth, his chill intelligence?
Sometimes I feel that I am their chosen insect, hopping
from day to night to day.
Just look at my wings, dividing light into its many selves.

If I'm nothing, I guess I want to be Their nothing,
not the nothing of the Daily News and the daily commute.
I made my choice, I can't remember how long ago –
maybe that's what it means to be chosen –
and here I am, brilliant, hurtful, suspicious and beloved,
dark body reflecting some distant, unapproachable light.

Spelling Bee

Twenty kids fidgeted on folding chairs, a sign
around each neck with name and school.
"Infinitesimal." When someone missed,
he had to remove his sign. "Synthesis."
The announcer repeated the word, gave
a definition, repeated it again. It wasn't fair!
A thousand years of dictionary against
one 12-year-old. "S - i - n," I began,
but the man at the mike stopped me.

I dropped in my chair, tore off my sign.
All but one sat down, "chagrin"
coloring our faces rouge,
                             and I wanted to go back,
centuries ago, and re-write that first word book,
the one that condemned us ever after
to struggle with impossible combinations,
like mages huddled over recipes for the afterlife.
Already I felt like Cain circling the walls
of Eden, my kind banished to a life of hard labor.

"Masculine, Summer, Wet"

Bottle flies humming on the back porch,
hospital refrigerators stacked with blood.

Outside, the air smothers
like a down comforter.

Remember Job, that just man,
favored of God, covered with boils.

Whatever I thought about leaves
wasn't large enough.

Crickets. Swallows. Mown
grass scented with mold. Bio-mass.

Black flies mumbling
like a priest over the Eucharist.

It's still day, and I'm trapped
in this refrigerator called a house.

A curse,
a temporary curse that night will ease

with her cool washcloth
and chilly, eternal eyes.

Let me suffer then,
the restless leaves converting

light into sugar,
waiting for the chance to breathe.

To the Teenager I Nearly Hit On Fairfax

You've done this dozens of times –
        falling off the curb with your buddies
like a trio of empty trashcans
        blown by winter

into the path of oncoming traffic –
        trucks full of gardeners from East L.A.,
mothers with infants strapped into their SUV's,
        hotheads in BMW's gunning for the freeway –

and had them stop short, like a heart
        whose pacemaker battery just expired.
Oh, you felt good, didn't you, Three Wise Men
        in your sweats of Emerald, Ruby, & Gold

on your way to buy Cokes or play b-ball or just hang out,
        some African flag come to life
& out there in the street waving its come-hither
        to herds of killer horse power.

Oh, I've been there too
        daring the world to run me over,
cops with bullhorns, soldiers with bayonets fixed,
        Presidents who thought my life was theirs to lose.

And guess what, they didn't bother
        to wipe the tear gas from my eyes
or lift me gently from in front of the troop train
        or halt the truncheon in its downward arc.

So this time I'm not stopping either,
        not even slowing down.
In fact, you'll see me speed up
        so that when I miss you, by inches,

you'll look up, maybe, & know there's something out here
        that wants to play your game,
and when it beats you,
        you hurt all the way to the grave.

Rocket 88

> *There's more than a touch of tomorrow in the Rockets of today*
> Oldsmobile marketing slogan

How I hated my father's unbending hardtop,
stubborn un-covertible,
stupid earthbound spaceship.

All aspiration, I ached
to rise above water, earth, & air
into the fiery furnace.

Like Icarus, like Phaeton,
I hungered for curved vistas,
an eagle's vision, a cosmonaut's.

I knew that only fire could propel me
into the kingdom of fire where Jesus
spoke with tongues of flame!

Every day, it seemed, new prophets rose,
astronauts with their squeezable stew,
their Tang, and anti-grav lavs,

untouched by their travels,
pencils and dandruff afloat
in dirty, recycled air,

while homebound I leaned on a fender
gazing skyward, bent backward,
a small tree snapped by Pentecostal winds.

Mantis In Spring

It is always spring for the mantis,
hope gushing from some pheromone fountain
inside its tiny brain. I found two
of them decorating my picket fence
like one of those wire sculptures
of hillbilly fiddlers you buy at Stuckey's
to hand to your sister-in-law
along with a pound of peanut brittle.
All afternoon they stood there,
tiny he mounting giant her,
like a boy trying out a new jungle gym.
I returned every hour and still
they were locked in embrace, consumed
with propagating their matchstick race.
But at what price? In late afternoon,
I saw his head was gone, her mandibles
clenching. They say he keeps on living,
his racing heart pumping sperm
with extra force. She dismembered him,
top down, like a child unbuilding a robot.
So this is one kind of love, a death
sentence with every declaration
of undying passion. I know it's just
instinct, and we're better than that,
but I can't help seeing myself in this *tableau
mordant*, disappearing like a saint
into the leonine maw of my first wife,
what started as something Rubenesque whittled
to a Giacometti tangle after years of gnawing.
And then I see that I'm the midget carnosaur,
blankly jawing my own small life.

Myopia

I have lost sight
of the middle distance
a range of burning hills
dust rising like fog
across a highway

I offer my hand
to the emptiness
in front of me

A branch scratches
the roof overhead
Something is trying
to get into this small life

I imagine walking
out the door into a sea of grass
Birds swim the warm current
Wind threshes the stalks

Useless vision
I would not know
how to use such freedom

Crickets scritch a washtub melody
Cornflowers dance on their stems

Even the dying mind
casts its seed

A Habit Of Ascent

Childhood, the first eternity,
as I wandered our vast acre,
trying to escape the sun.

How lonely it seemed with no children
nearby, just my sister, an insistent mouth
at mother's troubled breast.

The catalpas fanned heart-shaped leaves like aunts
trying to save their powder from streaking.
No clambering into their narrow laps.

The pear oozed like a teenager
craggy with acne, its bark a magnet
for columns of rock-climbing ants.

I circled the firs, transplanted
Christmas trees, shaggy and dangerous
as bears fattening for winter,

and stroked the knees of elm and oak,
giants chatting absent-mindedly
as the wind riffled their hair.

Only the apple, grandmother tree, my refuge
from the sky's enormous flame, was short and broad
enough to harbor this restless climber.

A cool green fire ignited her in spring
when I climbed into flowered lace
and huddled in the second crook, watching

leaves, then apples sweeten on stems.
Here where all the trouble began,
in the garden of the heart,

russet caterpillars drilled homes in green apples.
At night I dreamed the whole miracle again,
an explosion of green branching

into darkness, and yet I wanted more,
some escape from what I was,
from what my parents wanted me to be.

Come morning I'd drape myself along a limb
like a python, inhale the husky perfume,
the swollen fruit, as if this had always been my home.

René and the Fly

The room was growing
warm enough that languid flies
could rise and spiral
above the drowsing *philosophe*,
watching as if from great
distance the small, winged
bodies circling discretely
like numbers
in a celestial dance,

his mind lifting from the bed
as if to trace a parabola
toward some predestined
landing before expanding
exponentially,
its concussive burst
toppling churches and towers
as easily as if they were toys
brushed by some boy's
careless hand.

Fifth-Year Latin

Father Napoli stuffs his gooey hanky
into the sleeve of his cassock and points to
his next victim. Horace on the pleasures
of the simple life is anything but simple.

Even those of us with trots mangle the lines.
Father bends over his desk, sweating
and scanning the text, listening for mistakes.
His glasses ease down his Tuscan nose.

Every few minutes he returns them to their perch
with his middle finger. We are shocked, outraged,
and giggle at his innocence. Dyed hair rims
his tonsure like a hula dancer's skirt.

We wonder if we'll always be as strange
as we are now, or grow into the strangeness
he's become. Outside dust rises in thermals
from the soccer field. Runnels of sweat

pool in our crotches. We sweeten like grapes
on the ancient vines of Latium.

The Grove

— Cape Perpetua, Oregon

Like children huddled
        beneath a blanket, intent on
                their own secrets

and whispered charms,
        oblivious to the chill
                of grownup conversation,

its sometimes furious
        storms, these dwarves
                have turned their backs

on the ocean, their vivacious
        and voluble step-mom.
                Squat as four-year-olds

in shoulder pads
        they crowd and jostle
                just inches from the cliff.

They know they will
        never grow like their cousins
                in sheltered inland valleys,

the giant Spruce and Fir.
        Modesty, maybe, leaves them almost speechless
                except in the fiercest blow

when a sort of laughter
        flies from them, the only ones small enough
                to stand up to the weather.

Yellow Jacket

Thief and convict,
rising from your
hideout like smoke
from blackened ground.
Oh, to forage bracken
and mallow as if
that were enough
sweetness. To sink
into a pie's ruby
marsh. You wield
your knife like a kid
on a playground. Stab
and stab again. Hunger
drives you and the hum
of summer's fire, you
its sharpest spark. No
placket or gold buttons,
form-fitting shirt of
chitin, my chest x-ray,
my cracked ribcage and
defiant pact with life.

In the Nursery Of Priests

Drunk again on altar wine, I veer like a rudder
torn from a sinking boat, down the vaulted hall
where my fellow seminarians sleep their innocence away.

Close behind, I feel the Shadow, the one we call Lucifer,
an errant gust of light. Close, like in the library,
as I conjured the juju of my Latin texts,
trying to turn leaden me into gold,

and in the rec room – the click of billiard balls,
the clunk of Coke bottles, black tongues thrust from the lips
of the soda machine – this is his world as much as mine.

He invented internal combustion, wife-swapping and the tutu.
And though I long to hurl myself upstream past pools
of motor oil and condoms, I know I am a hooked bluegill,
his barb flashing in my mouth like motel neon.

The Sauna

A row of clay goblins molded
by some careless 3-year-old,
we sit on wooden racks
in our Swedish kiln,
a ruddy patina of sweat
coating our torsos.
Gravity has had its usual
simplifying effect, reducing
us to a squat and uniform
pudginess, we who were so proud
of our vaulted chests,
the well-turned metal of biceps
and thigh. Who would recognize
us from our yearbook?
Not our current crop of wives.
Not even classmates, absent
thirty years. Only our parents,
there at the beginning,
who could not stay for the end.
And ourselves, aggrieved
at time's heedless insult
to our once flagrant beauty.

Snake Skin

Crotalus atrox
(Diamondback rattlesnake)

A strip of paper curls in shattered grass,
pebbled skin printed slant.
Why am I so shaken,
imagining a torqued body rearing?
This is only parchment –
a body's history and testament –
not the raptured strike.

Such death dealing beauty –
Navajo and Hopi knew how to draw
its power, bands of black diamonds
on rug and umber pot.

From creosote brush, tinder-ready
in the canyon below,
comes the rattle's distant warning,
and I am reassured.
We are not at war.

I raise the husk in sharp twilight,
wind it round my arm –
dressing some untreated wound.

Leaving Tracks

Once upon a
million years ago,
A. Afarensis,*
the petite and hairy
mother of us all,
walked the shore of
Tanganyika's
lake, leaving a trail
in newly fallen
volcanic ash.
This morning I followed
my 2-year-old's
muddy prints
from the lettuce patch
into her mother's kitchen,
each shapely step
fainter than the last,
the way we'd lose track
of our great grand ape
were it not for the fossil
trace of her broad feet,
the load-bearing
arches which held her
almost erect, and
her ten pretty toes.

* Australopithecus Afarensis, an early hominid ancestor of modern H. Sapiens

The Great Circle

At Stonehenge chrome stanchions
hold hands around the perimeter
like a cordon of tiny Bobbies guarding the P.M.,

but at Avebury you can touch the stones,
follow the sheep, or have your picture taken
with a Druid. The Druids are nice,

white-haired and draped in homespun.
They smile as if they've seen it all.
Is it strange I find the sheep –

in their pre-shrunk, all-weather
Captain's sweaters – more admirable
and worthy of imitation?

Before slaves had hewn the first megalith
and dragged it from some distant quarry,
there were sheep in this meadow

investigating clover, taking notes on dozens
of species of grass, casting their fecal grapeshot
like handfuls of wedding rice.

I wonder if they notice the wonders
of this place, the giant stones and ditch,
the putative astronomy – these outsized works

of man. When we scatter in our Euro-coupes
to tasty teas of scones and jam, they will still be here,
students of the weather, the never-ceasing,
unrepeatable motions of light and air.

Early Space Travel

I take my son into the dusk
under trees still heavy
with the season's first rain.

We watch as the entire
face of the moon darkens,
like a child with a bad cold.

I show him – my right hand,
the earth, hides my left, the moon,
from the sun, my son.

He has a book which shows
the solar system so he knows
that the moon rotates around the earth,

just as the mom orbits the son.
"Where is the earth?" he wants
to know. "Which earth?" I ask.

"The one in the sky," he says,
pointing at an invisible planet
in the fragrant emptiness

beyond the trees, the one
blocking the sun's light
and giving the moon a chill.

"You're standing on it," I say.
He looks at me, perhaps wondering
if all adults lie so easily.

Letter To a Grandchild

After the first freeze you pick your way among leaves' confetti.
Yesterday's puddles are still there, still water, only slick now and hard.

You prise a milky muscle, intact from its abattoir of insects and leaves,
asking if those smeared rainbows stretched on its surface were always
       there.

You raise the false mirror – rose window of memory – to your face
and regard the sun, low to the smudged horizon, how diamonds gather

at its focal point. Hold this moment close until your nose burns with
       frostbite.
Not even snow driving sideways can make you forget the light you see

moving behind the surface of things, the universe expanding like your
       breath
to the immense dimensions inside your small dark head.

Daddy Long Legs

High in a corner of the baby's room a shred of silk,
what a fisherman might find in the wake of a speedboat,
lopsided slub from ceiling to wall,
yet luffing with every step I take, creation's most tattered sail.
And near the wall, its burden, a knot,
the egg sac's bulging belly.
How soon will this smidgen of cream boil to a glassy froth?

And where is the mother? There. At eye level.
A strider on stilts, eight-eyed, poisonous maybe,
as far from human as animal gets.

Father, mother, both trying to survive,
we stare, caught in the net which snares us all.

Camping On the Big Sur

Through an aisle of redwoods
in the cathedral of Big Sur
I bear a steaming liter of piss
to the toilets, my chalice
a child's potty, a tomato red plastic
bowl for mixing the sacred
and profane. Like a priest
hurrying the forbidden host
down Communist streets, I pass
a neighbor, exhaling incense
into amniotic light,
his first cigarette of the day,
and notice how it mingles
with ammonia rising
ghostly from liquid gold.

With no water for cleaning,
survivors at Auschwitz
were the ones who washed
in the body's brine, sterile
despite the smell. How it
must've repelled their captors,
those acrid faces, the vivid,
perfumed scalps, gleaming like
the delivery room floor when the sac
burst – and then my daughter came,
after months in that hidden sea.
Strolling back to the tent, I shake
the last drops from the pan, as if
in blessing, through woods filled
with the cries of children and birds.

The Matter Of the Caterpillar

The world of the caterpillar is a jar
and a few snatches of grass
wadded from the lawn.

A many-jointed finger,
she leans green racing stripes
against her wrap-around window.

If I placed the jar, skylights in its metal roof,
in the middle of a leisurely pasture
flecked with cowpies in the deep hills

of Minnesota, say, how many
ghosts would gather to the jar –
yellow jackets, sweat bees, dragonflies?

If only my caterpillar did not beckon so,
if only, lingering, every cell
longed for transparency,

that glassy state
through which information passes
with only the smallest distortion –

and yet this singular digit
climbs the wall – her every molecule
yearning to rise into the dangerous air

and, self propelled, strain
abstract light
through time-stained wings.

RECIPES FOR THE AFTERLIFE

Pantoumime

A producer took my pantoum to lunch.
He's on his own now and needs a free meal –
at least that's what he says – and he talks a lot –
he's got this compulsion to repeat himself.

He's on his own now so he needs a free meal
and someone to listen while he complains
about his compulsion to repeat himself.
It's hard for him to meet girls when all he wants

is someone to listen while he complains
about being the river that runs beneath the river.
It's hard to meet girls when all they want
is a pretty boy gazing in a pool

where the river that runs beneath the river
suddenly surfaces. He wants to say,
I'm more than a pretty boy gazing in a pool.
I'm the shadow that refuses to lie down

and suddenly surfaces in what you say.
I'm the reverses you suffer looking in a mirror,
the shadow (there I go again) that refuses to lie down,
the echo when you have nothing to say.

You suffer, don't you, when you look in the mirror
and there's nothing to say, not even an echo.
That's what he said he said – and he talks a lot –
the producer who took my pantoum to lunch.

Sadao S. Munemori Memorial Interchange

Where the 405 sweeps westward to join the 105
   in its progress to the sea, a ghost building
      rises from the grass of sadness,

home to ethereal dentists and accountants,
   virtual computer salesmen and spirit janitors.
      It mirrors its twin to the south

in everything but reality. Flattened
   in the name of speed, it disappeared
      like nearby houses & storefront churches,

as transient as any grove of scrub oak.
   Nothings lasts, & in LA it lasts even less.
      I see this in my midnight mirror,

how I've gratefully suffered
   the sun's combustion, an anorexic
      flame leaning into the dark.

The Road To Emmaus

How many feet have scuffed this track
to such a polish? My brother and I
wince when we look down. The burnt recesses
of hills, even the scumbled roadside
makes us squint in the all-present glare.
Inward, I long to go there, a cool
cave where the mind eases like a trickle
of water along the deepest wall. What are we
fleeing? And who is this man who insists
on joining us? A spy? How watchful he is.
And yet if I tried to describe him, I could not.
He seems the double of this unyielding country.
Friends await us. But will we reach them?
Some terror, still hidden, mimics our steps.

Space Walk With Turkeys

Motel sex, no matter how good with your own wife,
is better with someone else's, the ghosts
of all those horny strangers, a cheering section
of lingering sweetness, infecting the sheets.

30 minutes north of the Johnson Space Center,
I was watching football and thinking of the Mrs.
back home. Outside, the interstate
vibrated with the hum of livestock trailers.

The other woman, angry now, was also out there
in the sauna of South Texas.
I could've followed her but how could I face
the weather, drenching the plains with brutal light.

News flash – guys in space suits were performing
an EVA in a giant herd of turkeys.
Some alien strain had gotten into one
and so they all had to die. I turned off the sound

and tried to imagine every inch of the thousand
miles that separated me from my vows,
all the sagebrush and motels,
that turkey farm almost across the road.

I wondered if it would be better to wait
and see which of the offended spouses
would burst through the door
and fill me with enough lead to open

my own ammo dump, or should I stroll
under the overpass to witness the death
of 10,000 innocents,
whether by gas, lethal injection, or machine gun?

Not since Antietam would so many die
so quickly on American soil.
When I was a kid, I fed the chickens –
a lesser species, I'll admit, than the noble turkey –

but they died singly, honorably,
my mother's hands wringing their throats.
Somewhere beneath the sorghum
stretching in every direction, a couple

of Air Force uniforms manned radar & red phones,
the Phi Beta key of destruction dangling from their necks.
Meanwhile their Russian counterparts crouched below
the wheat fields of Ukraine. I was tired

of ignoring them, tired of pretending
that tomorrow I might be alive.
I wanted to say something rude to the hucksters
of honorable death. But this was Texas,

where justice comes flying at you like an ICBM.
I swear, I could almost hear the groan
of those death row turkeys
as they watched their executioners,

men suffocating in rubber suits,
wade across that rapidly evaporating sea of birds.

On Poverty

O Mother of Disease and Ignorance
   and a thousand other brats, who loves you now?
You loot the public treasury and lance
   our swollen self-esteem, that fatted cow.
I've seen you sitting on a stoop surrounded
   by your brood, their sleepy hooded eyes
     that track each well-fed passer-by in his car,
        and heard your baby's hungry cries
   as it lay in bed and one more day rounded
     into darkness, one more wound into scar.

Once you were a nun, by all respected,
   at home among the ill, the lame, the blind,
and though you cared for all, went uninfected,
   by abstract vigors of the mind.
I've seen you kneel in some grave sanctuary,
   fat beeswax flames enlightening the gloom,
     head bent, hands folded, swallowed by quimnet
        as you pondered mankind's doom
   and held an easy, heart-felt colloquy
     with God, your refuge from earthly riot.

But though I've seen you haggard and serene,
   I've always known your beauty, O bright star,
and loved you, my ever difficult queen,
   intimately, from afar.
Each taste of cool water tastes of you.
   You are the clarity of a wind-bright day,
     you the sweetness of berries plumped in mud.
        How could I doubt your love for me,
   stronger than my fear, who does not cease to woo,
     your voice, the ancient murmur of the blood?

Lessons In Sushi

The grandson of a Buddhist abbot taught me what little I know about
>   how to order – start simple, two thin slices of *maguro* on
>   fingerlings of sticky rice, a smear of *wasabi*, pungent as a
>   punch in the nose. Every day I'd sit at my desk and pretend
>   I could balance the demands of commerce and friendship.
>   The Director of a language school, I was supposed to figure
>   out how to pay teachers and bills,

but all I wanted was to teach. My wife was proud of me. For the first
>   time in our marriage I was making more money. I forgot the
>   *miso*. Before any fish you need to wash away the taste of the
>   day, fermented soybean paste in broth. Our marriage was
>   in constant danger, and we liked it that way, peering from a
>   rooftop bar into the Basin, bits of hillock and highrise
>   floating in a brown petrochemical soup.

After *maguro*, you might try a more flavorful or fatty fish, yellowtail
>   or *toro*. I'm not sure about *toro*, just as I'm not sure when the
>   abbot's grandson stopped being a student and became our
>   friend. For years my wife and I played the open-marriage
>   game as if we both could be winners. When he ran out of
>   money, I let him teach me Japanese instead of paying tuition.

On weekends our new friend Kei tried to teach us *mah-jongg*, pastime
>   of warriors and spies. Maybe I could have been better at it, but
>   I couldn't enjoy winning when losing caused her so much
>   pain. Every Friday we'd drop thirty bucks in a sushi bar, which
>   back then was a lot. Between courses you were supposed to
>   napalm your tongue with *sake* or a beer, but Ke preferred hot
>   tea, *ocha*,

first cousin to what grandpa served in the monastery to keep his
>   monks awake on their cushions late at night. Back then some
>   Air Force guy, a hero to a lot of Americans, declared that
>   we should bomb our enemy back to the Stone Age (I forget
>   which enemy, we had so many) – or maybe he said we
>   needed to destroy some country

in order to save it. I didn't like to admit it, but I agreed, as if I were the country in question. Thank God sushi was simpler. After *toro*, something salty or sweet, roe or crispy eel skin smeared with teriyaki sauce. Kei had thick hair, a round peasant face, and stocky build. He ran around the park every evening, following the groove left by other runners, sometimes

running the whole way backwards, because it worked different muscles and because he wanted to challenge himself. He loved us both, I think, and we loved the challenge of our difficult relationship, built on suspicion and distrust, the pain reminding us we were still alive. We were bored – who in their thirties isn't, with so much time to kill before death. Whenever he'd visit, he left his shoes at the door

and bowed, like someone entering a holy place. I felt sorry for her, I felt sorry for them both. Don't think that makes me a nice guy. I wanted to make her happy, but couldn't do it by myself. I liked to say she was touring the world in bed, first a Syrian, and later an African, and finally an East Asian. It was cruel, but the best jokes usually are. So I let him,

in his entirely innocent and honorable way, sleep with her. Feeling sorry for myself was as natural as chewing, but how could I tell him that my job, my life were beginning to swallow me? When I learned enough to order sushi, I quit the lessons. She loved it when I ordered – *Ocha o, kudasai!* – reciting the utterly foreign sounds as if I knew something

worth knowing. Finally we stopped seeing him, and he went back to his country, and I left her for another woman. I haven't mentioned dessert, *tamago*, paper-thin slices of egg welded into an omelette – sugar and horseradish colliding on the tongue like radioactive isotopes. The only thing I'm sure of is I loved them both.

Mother Tongue

*(An Italian-American soldier guards internees
on the trip from Oakland to Crystal City, Texas)*

In the half light of the second-class car,
the faces of jostled sleepers gleamed like mushrooms
in the leafy undergrowth of their clothes.
He remembered the sour smell of mould
and fish guts along the muddy banks
of the Wolf River, his line taut in the cold
brightly wrinkled flood. He didn't know about
the other camps, six thousand miles away,
"factories of death." Sometimes he worried
that the prisoners would give him trouble.
The little kids were worst.
He was used to dealing with trouble
in small doses, a glass-jawed middleweight
with a good right cross or some cocky recruit
who knew too many slurs for Italians.
Nobody likes a fight. Not even fighters.
He patted his Smith and Wesson
as another small town smear of light glazed
the windows. As a boy he'd seen bloody-
aproned butchers put a gun to a cow's
temple, watched the muzzle explode,
blood rivering from mouth and nose.
He knew how savage those Southern boys could be,
and yet he was glad that *nonno* had left
the old country, glad he was not dying
for *la patria* on some dusty hill.
All day the bronze train flowed past switching
yards and naked buttes rusting in the sun.
The cruelest landscapes he had ever seen
swallowed them, reducing them to nothing.
He tried not to think of his own skin
darkening in the muggy fields back home.
Tried not to see his mother's pale lips
speaking the language of the enemy.

After Spicer

the heart is a rose pierced by a stone
the heart has porcelain handles
and wheels of finest silk
the heart cries like an actor
playing his final role
an aging drunken poet
charming one last loveboy

the walls of the heart are pricked by stars
the drunken eyes of animals open
and close like fists pounding
plastic barstools
the heart is schooled in restraint
the heart is cool to all
but its own lethargies, its own leather swelling

the heart's some dickhead
pretending to be a poet
won't somebody take the poor dickhead
home for the night?
the heart stumbles into the mouths
of animals, the meat of their passion
passing into sweet, deliberate song

A Poet

> *The vision makes him yearn inside himself.*
> *It makes him mourn.*
>   – John Logan

He has a boy's gift for error
and hope. He fiddles with his glasses
as if disappointed in what he sees.
No matter how strong the prescription
he knows he will never find the necessary
quiddity. There is truth, though, in
this other glass, chalice filled
with scotch, collecting all that is gold
in the twilight into its chill self.
He pauses to admire its selfless composition
of chair and sofa, gold shirt, gold face,
and high-ceilinged windows shadowed
by the living world.

He had dreamed of purity but gotten this
embarrassment of wives and children and
friends of his small fame.
Was he the man who'd said,
"The poet is a god, his creation
more necessary than the 'merely real.'"

Drinking alone is like writing, he thinks,
a pleasure made sweet by selfishness.
He holds the glass with both hands
as an altar boy holds a candle,
a candle which burns at wavelengths
sensible only to the nose, slowly
exhausting the room's oxygen.

Everything leads him back to death.
It is his science and complaint.
He conjures the dead to tell him
what he already knows and refuses

to believe. They stand there chatting
as at a party, hands by their sides
with nothing to hold. They eye him
tenderly, as if remembering his sweetness
as a child, his gentleness with pets,
the way he guarded his sister.
They are waiting for him to join them,
waiting to gather his immense and frustrated love
into the darkness pouring into the room.

Almost Icarus

> "About suffering they were never wrong,
> the Old Masters."
> — W. H. Auden

Well, almost never. We admire their sense
of proportion, how small suffering looks
when placed in this indifferent
lovely world of ours. And their calm,
how they enjoy sunshine on leaves
and windows, how the ripples
of a personal calamity are swallowed
by some uniformly wrinkled sea.

They remind us, for our own good, of
how we look to mountains and clouds.
How dare we correct them? And yet we do
every day, preferring the close-up
& quick cut to the establishing shot.

This afternoon a boy, having come perhaps
to the center of the maze of his life, climbed
to the roof of a four-story building, and jumped.
I don't know if he meant to fall to the asphalt below
or instead intended to catch with his arms' thin
struts and meager wingflesh the insistently blue breeze
which hurled itself against that precipice

of brick and glass. For the loiterers and tourists,
the musicians and massage therapists,
it was a break, who knows how welcome,
from their routine, and they flocked to the fallen figure.
I didn't have to guess what they were thinking.
I heard a woman on her cell, " . . . just the junkie
in the basement . . . yeah, the one who keeps hitting
on my brother," and a blonde man asked,

"Did somebody tell him to jump?" & another
in the chorus, with sideburns and tattoos,
called, "Hell yes, I told him to jump!"

But then, as we clustered like bits of metal
welded by a powerful magnet
into one thing, the crowd grew silent,
straining for a glimpse of that body,
its imperfect beauty as fragile as our own.
There was nothing to say, or do, except
acknowledge the logic of gravity and part
like trees before bulldozers when the
paramedics came. It was a beautiful
afternoon, we all knew it, which nothing,
not even this, could totally spoil.

Every Anger Has a Voice

Welcomed by chattering iron teeth,
a jittery V-Dub veers into the parking lot,
slows at the guard shack and speed bumps,
but barely, before filling an empty slot.

The Senior Systems Analyst uncoils himself
onto the asphalt, his hand still curled
after the long drive around a cigarette,
only to recoil from a shadow plummeting

from a light pole. A mockingbird screeches
like a car alarm & swoops past, stirring nicotine
plumes. Should he wait it out, or, *oh fuck it*,
he says, out again and slamming the door,

hand raised against the sun or the bird
or his own anger. For every anger has a voice,
whether it screams like the burning star
overhead or roars like dinosaurs

in the scrapyard next door or fumes
like the cracking plant across the freeway
or groans like that never-ending river of cars
always at flood. Or maybe it's a six-inch

dive bomber, insignia bright as smog,
that can, it seems, imitate whatever it hears,
squeaky gate, a dog barking, the soul
battling to enter the mouth where it belongs.

The Monk and the Killer Chickens

It's an hour before dawn when I shuffle
into the meditation hall and find a cushion.

Redwoods weep on the corrugated roof.
Smoke from a distant forest drifts from the altar.

I settle into the ache in my knees,
tendons humming like piano wire.

I don't know what's missing from my life.
Maybe not looking will help me find it.

It's dark outside, but I can hear
roosters crowing across the road.

They never sleep
and are always asking for a fight,

pit bulls with feathers.
The local farmers need a bumper crop

to pay for their tennis courts and jacuzzis,
so if it's not cannabis, it's fighting cocks,

a thousand bucks a bird in Bangkok, home
of child prostitutes and Buddha's devoutest devotees.

Why did the chicken refuse to cross the road?
He was waiting for a limo to take him to the airport.

I wonder what I'm waiting for, a chariot,
something to fight for?

At night I lie in my tent and listen to rounds
from a thirty-aught-six echo like tennis balls

in the vast and looming hills. I dream that I'm
a chicken, razor blades tied to my spurs,

tiny brain seething with adrenalin. Was it karma
put birds and monks so close, Zen flowing

into this country, chickens flying out,
balancing the trade between East and West?

"I and the Village"

       Marc Chagall, 1911

This paradisal moment will not die,
nor will the stars above the yellow dome.
The green man and the calf meet eye to eye.

A she-goat casts her likeness on the sky,
the child who milks her smaller than a womb.
This paradisal moment will not die.

A girl waits upside down. A man with scythe
trudges, face averted, through the loam.
The green man and the calf meet eye to eye.

What does it see, with iris moon on high,
and he, with sun that shines like honeycomb?
That this paradisal moment soon will die?

Due north the city where the Tsar will lie,
the Revolution come; and here the tomb
where green man and calf meet eye to eye.

History, they say; more than that, say I,
if love of white for red and black still bloom,
this paradisal moment will not die –
green man and calf meet eye to eye.

"Figure With Meat"

The museum tea room was full of bare-headed daughters
and mothers in large pale hats. It was the pastel
decade. My sandwich, cut into four

equilateral triangles, surrounded a perfect
dome of potato salad, my father's bald head.
It was the decade of long-line panty girdles

and stockings that whispered when you walked.
We sat next to the reflecting pool where I could see myself,
already tall and lean with no loveliness to spare.

My mother talked the whole time about how nice
my dress looked, her voice like a fork clattering on china,
but I was lost in my reflected self,

a watery blonde with stringy hair.
Maybe I was drunk on hair spray and the scent of Chanel
rubbing against all those White Shoulders,

for when we entered the gallery, I saw a portrait
in lurid blues and blacks, slabs of bacon or beef
grotesque with pain, yet familiar, human as breakfast.

Do I need to say I was unable to look away?
My mother led me from the room like some kind stranger
must have led the zealot Saul

after he had fallen from his horse,
blind with a vision only he could see,
his heart a confusion of beauty and murder.

"Philip Sleeping"

I depict his back because my husband's face
with its abstract, New England
simplicity of shadow and line

would distract from the torso's
weathered creams and blues,
its muscled marble. Notice,

I've confined him to the leftmost
third of the canvas, while the rest,
a seascape of pillows and sheets

tossed by a passing squall, declares
that someone has just left, maybe me
but more likely, one of the women or men

whose need for his beauty is more physical
than mine. Whoever it is, I want you to feel
him – solid, opaque, unmoved.

You will say, perhaps, the work seems cool
and think to yourself *cruel, a bit callous,*
a child worrying some belovéd pet.

But who will remember what he was
when all the world desired him?
How vivid the bedclothes, how restless,

breaking in waves against his dreaming form.

Discobolos

Do you remember that day on Rhodes,
the picture you took? The rough seas
at the end of summer had made you sick,

so when the boat parked in the last port
in Europe, and we boarded a bus to another *petit*
Parthenon, a hilltop ruin strewn with the island's

granite molars, you weren't happy.
It was hot. The sun ricocheted off the sea
like a volley of bees, and I was being silly.

Maybe it was the ouzo for lunch,
cloudy with ice, a fogbank,
herald of oncoming winter,

or maybe the tipsy joy
of being your husband.
So there I crouched on a slab

of marble in my 50-year-old skin,
coiled like time itself before it starts
to run down, gripping my past,

the heaviest thing I carried,
like an invisible discus behind my back,
about to fling that magic rock forever

into the brilliant, blinding blue,
where it would sink as surely as Icarus,
who dared the gods and lost.

"Rockefeller's Teeth"

Along the harbor with its view of conifered flat and hill,
the late summer crowds stream from shop to faded shop.
The poor among them have a choice of t-shirts designed
and fabricated in China – puffins proud of their singular
beaks, the familiar outline of the seven glacier-scraped
mountains, sailboats rotting gaily at anchor, or in rain-
bow script, just the name itself, *Bar Harbor*, like a foghorn's
one insistent note, re-formed and embellished by the fog.

Children scream outside the hand-made ice cream store
and teenagers wander in the park, boldly kissing away
their boredom, while we middle-aged art lovers stroll
among boutiques and remember the view from Mount
Cadillac, its godlike vista of islands amid the all-consuming
sea, and our bracing walk around Jordan Pond,
followed by the artful counterpoint of tea and popovers
consumed on the long green lawn stretching to the lake.

What did they call them, those cairns, mini-megaliths
which line the carriage paths? The workmen who quarried
them on site, Irish and Italians who came here
from Boston and New York, for, what, six or seven
summers, and never came again, to build this playground
for Rockefeller and his new friends, the Winslows and Lowells,
the Vanderbilts and Eliots? No need for *riche* and
nouveau riche to hike or climb the hills and forests.

To encounter nature they needed only step into
their phaetons to view the shedding oak
and alder gathered in penitential groves
and trembling like the urban poor in winter.
Their sturdy horses pulled them up the gentle grade
to the only heights, besides their new skyscrapers,
which measured their self-made eminence,
and from which they might savor in that vivid scene

their own granite will, the capacious reach of their power,
while on either side, those rows of nameless
head stones, those tablets waiting for new
commandments, stretched like a giant's mouth,
the mouth of the new century, the mouth of capitalism
itself, which having swallowed immigrant workers,
was even then grinding them with mis-matched
molars and cunningly angled canines.

Or so it might seem, a century gone, to those who
look down on that great selfishness, a man, say,
and his wife, she descended from the phaetons,
he a cousin of the huddled mass, neither
of them desperately poor or despicably rich,
solid around the middle as they undoubtedly are,
visitors to this place where once their ancestors
contended in polite and undeclared war.

They are just tourists in a forgotten history,
residents of a crowded present, common as leaves
ratcheting in the breeze. Who remembers what
happened, Love, or how it felt when the only
answer to unchecked wealth was scorn disguised
as jest? And what is this mystery which knits unequals
into a whole? The forest flutters its many tongues
bidding goodbye to everything but this moment.

In the Sculpture Garden

These figures of metal and stone
aren't frozen. They move, just more slowly

than we ephemerals. That family
with their large granite bodies

and tiny heads probably think of the rock
on which they sit as some kind of pet,

breathing and shifting at their own tranquil rate.
And this nude, female "River," cascading

imperceptibly into a lotus pond, she's
been flowing for almost a hundred years,

yet hasn't lost more than a instant
of the eternity with which she began.

The crowd circles with a drowsy murmur
like flies drowning in summer's heat.

A boy and a girl are playing "statue,"
their hands wrapped around each other's necks.

The bronze ballerina beside me
stands as securely *en pointe* as she did

in the *fin de siecle*. Her ruffled skirt
breathes with the seasons, and I,

smitten with the voluptuous emptiness
of her calves, am almost a statue too.

What am I waiting for, some cue
from the wind to lift her? How long

have I known this moment would come
when I would meet my mother as a young girl,

still hopelessly in love with her life, my
father trilling unseen in the skirt of a tree.

About the Author

Lee Rossi was born in St. Louis, Missouri. He studied 5 years for the Roman Catholic priesthood before leaving the seminary. He has published two ESL textbooks, as well as a critical study of C.S. Lewis and J.R.R. Tolkien. He is the author of two previous books of poetry, *Ghost Diary* (Terrapin Press, 2003) and *Beyond Rescue* (Bombshelter Press, 1992), and has appeared in various anthologies, including *Blue Arc West* (Tebot Bach, 2006), *Chance of a Ghost* (Helicon Nine Editions, 2005), *Mischief, Caprice, & Other Strategies* (Red Hen Press, 2002) and *Grand Passion: the Poetry of Los Angeles and Beyond* (Red Wind Books, 1995).

His poems, reviews and essays have been published in numerous journals, including *Tar River Poetry, The Atlanta Review, The Green Mountains Review, The Sun, Poetry East, Chelsea, The Wormwood Review, Nimrod, Beloit Poetry Journal, Poet Lore, and The Southern Poetry Review*. From 1986 to 1992, he edited *Tsunami*, a journal of contemporary poetry. He is Staff Reviewer and Interviewer for *Pedestal*.

He lives in California.

www.ingramcontent.com/pod-product-compliance
Lightning Source LLC
Chambersburg PA
CBHW052109070526
44584CB00017B/2401